MUTE

Words That Never Meant Anything to You

Moza Al Sharif

Published by Sail Publishing L.L.C.

First published in 2024

Copyright © 2024 by Sail Publishing L.L.C.

All rights reserved. This book or any portion thereof may not be reproduced or used in any manner whatsoever without the express written permission of the publisher except for the use of brief quotations in a book review.

This book uses a font and an alignment purposed to make the reading experience easier for dyslexics, towards an inclusive reading experience.

ISBN: 979-8-9893775-6-5

UAE National Media Council Permit #: MC-02-01-3006511

Age Classification: +16
The age classification for this book's contents is set in accordance with the age classification system issued by the UAE's National Media Council.

Email: info@SailPublishing.com
Facebook: facebook.com/SailPublishing
Instagram: @SailPublishing
Twitter: @SailPublishing

Contents

Introduction 4

I'm Done Talking 21

She Got the Memo 56

Bittersweet 87

Eye on the Target 106

Hello Stranger 123

Iyashi 142

Introduction

I spend most of my days at home. I could be reading, binge-watching a TV show, or maybe just lying in bed, staring at the ceiling, daydreaming of what my life could have been. On good days, I might take a walk outside and get my fair share of endorphins through the rays of sunlight reflecting upon my face as I hear the squeals of kids playing on the street. It feels nice to experience those simple things in life when you feel alone in a house full of people, which fascinates me if I'm going to be quite honest. What always seems to grab my attention whenever I take a short walk outside is the brown-feathered bird that tends to come over to the garden for some food my mother puts out for the birds every day. Why does she strike my interest, you ask? Because she's the only brown-feathered bird that visits, while the rest are a grayish color. I'm not very knowledgeable on what type of bird she is, but the color of her feathers makes her the minority of the flock, the odd one out. The other birds will not let her feast in peace. She's always in her corner, but she doesn't want to soar to a better destination, one where she feels welcomed. She prefers to stay here. She seems comfortable. Let's not disturb her. I think she might be trying to find some comfort from the blustery turbulence she faces every day. Oh, and I'm not talking about the wind. It's been quite calm these days. She reminds me of myself in a way.

Before we begin, I would like to thank everyone who has read my first book, *Moonlight Howl*, which is a dedication to my beloved sister. Ever since I gifted her the book, her overall state and well-being have blossomed. She has become the most loving sister with a beautiful free-spirited soul, and she continues to surprise me in many ways. I wouldn't have done it without your support, and so I thank you from the depths of my heart.

For now, let's focus on moving on to better days.

Shielded with a guard heightened towards the sky
And a cover much stronger than steel
She was so afraid of expressing her vulnerability
Because she was terrified of what it could do to her.
Once that guard breaks down
The overflow of murky water will smother her
And all the rocks and debris will shatter her bones
Making it feel like there's nowhere to go
And with her subdued voice
No one could ever hear her.
It feels like she is being attacked by sharks
Circling her until her last breath.

And don't get me started on the low tides of judgment that follow
She doesn't want to welcome them
They are an accessory she never wanted to wear.

Alienated in her zone
She just wanted to express herself freely.
But people's reactions towards her harsh life
Is what makes her prefer to shut up
As many have told her to do.

Some days it's only about reflection.
Just understanding how she feels
Was something she could never understand
Because she was hardly understood.

She never denied those feelings
Never rejected those thoughts
But she did not want to force unwanted conversations
Between her and her mind.

Long live the day
When she learned about acceptance
And the need to let go.
That day, she felt as free as one can be.

Learning to accept her past
And the ambiguity of her future
Did not only allow her to embrace the present moment
But pushed her to thrive at living every moment of it
While bracing every inch of what life can offer
Both good and bad.

Simply absorb the good
And let all the bad flow through you.

She always had this notion that she should stop talking
When it starts to feel like she is talking to a wall.
Do you get that too?

Just understand that you won't always be
Someone else's priority as they have been yours.
Learn this sooner than later.

She was always amused by the fact that she wore hoodies all the time
Stupid, I know...
But she did not do this because it was cold.

(This time we're not referring to her heart, I promise.)

It just made her feel secure.
Embraced by whom she loved in her imaginary world.
The warmth of it all.
Oh, the wonders of how the mind works.
When you see her in the midst of summer, coated heavily
Don't judge her.
She might just be having a hard time
And she just wants to feel safe and sound.

As a child,
She wasn't invited to most of her friends' birthday parties
And she never really understood why.

As a teenager,
She wasn't invited to her friends' graduation parties
And she thought about asking why.

As an adult,
She wasn't invited to her friends' weddings
And she never asked why.

She got the memo.

I think it's time
For her to learn
How to detach herself
From people and things
That no longer serve her
And her sanity.

A lot of things change
When you shift from being close to someone
To being just another acquaintance
From their standpoint
And only theirs.

Over the years she realized
Those unwanted hardships
Don't deserve an ounce of recognition.
But the positive challenges within those hardships
That serve her growth…
Those…
Those deserve her undivided attention.

She needed more time to find herself again
But she thought it was too late
After she hit 21 years of age.
She should have been
Planning a fancy brunch
An extraordinary wedding
Her first child's name
But that wasn't the case.

For now, she spends a lot of time making up
For what she missed when she was younger.
Being an adult at a young age wasn't fun at all.
But resolving childhood trauma in adulthood isn't so bad after all.
Focus on your own well-being
No matter what age you are.
Leave the rest for later.
It'll come.

She's 29 now
And good days *have been* coming for her more frequently.

Trying to hold back all the anger
All the built-up aggression
To not hurt anyone
Especially her loved ones.

What was she even thinking?
We're all living in an outraged world
And we're all trying to do the same thing: survive.

"You're so dramatic!"
That's all she needed to hear to stop expressing herself.

"You look funny when you cry… You should stop!"
Don't get me started on this one.
She never shed a tear after that.

She let's her body fall
Into the void
She doesn't know where she's going
But at least she's going somewhere.

She may have a lot of free time
But she's still busy
She occupies her time, drenched in thought
Reflecting
Understanding
Finding ways to become a better person
And she wishes everyone would do the same.

The first time she felt a sense of abandonment
Was when her best friend moved to a different city
With nothing but the frail landline connection between them.

They never tell you how to get by
When you're faced with the distance of a loved one
You must figure it out on your own.

She's currently a grown woman
With just a handful of friends
Because she's terrified of loss
And has no interest in meeting strangers
To befriend them.

I'm Done Talking

Here's some advice for those who don't feel heard. You can either take it or leave it. There are some people who might not be interested in hearing your stories, and there are others who would be willing to sit through an hour-long conversation just to listen to you talk about what has been crushing your soul. I can understand that on some days, you might feel like there is no one, because your troubles feel unresolvable, or maybe you just feel like a burden. The list of reasons why you may not want to speak up is as valid as your existence is today and every day. In the end, those who treat you like family, your real friends and I are just happy to see you alive and well. Make journaling your best friend if your voice isn't your strongest quality. No one can force you to speak, but you need to address your concerns in some way. I get that lonesome feeling on most days, like tonight, for instance. Tonight… tonight calls for some journaling. Let it all out, beautiful. Draw some petals around those teardrops on the page.

She's finding it quite hard
To meet your benchmark
And to possibly go beyond it.
Like a strenuous project
She cannot comprehend your requirements.
All those unerasable errors
Leaving no space for a second chance.
Just time and effort wasted
On a sentimental plan
Articulated to its core
Plainly cut into pieces
Crumpled in the palm of your hand
And thrown away.
In retrospect, she feels stupid.
She's sacrificing her own sanity
To please you
Just like a bad ritual.
But she learns from her mistakes.

She has no energy
To deal with those
Who have no energy
For her.

When you've been living a stressful life
And suddenly all the stress goes away
You kind of forget how to live.
If you're not stressing
You're stressing about why you're not stressing.

Live free, young one.

She schedules in a happy day
With a lot of exciting plans
But then one person turns up
To throw in a hurtful comment.
Then another person turns up
With a statement that crushes her soul.
And another
Who makes her question her presence in life.
They're like ants.
Once one sees the fruit
The rest keep coming.

Would anyone else like to ruin her day?

She mirrors back
Their own harsh actions
And now they're mad.

"Why is there so much pleasure in this?"
She asks as she laughs internally
With a mild smirk on her face.

At this moment in time
Don't try to save her
Just let her be.

She's just trying to find ways to express herself
And it's working.
It's finally working
Through the pages of this book.

From being the person dearest to her heart
To a person whom she could no longer tolerate,
Not even for one more second.

It's funny how she went back to being a stranger,
And how she likes it better this way.

Her mother always got her shoes
That tended to be tight on her feet
But she never made a fuss about it.
With a small built figure
She had to be the man of the house
The mother to her siblings
Smiling in every family occasion
To show that everything was going well
And to avoid any unwelcome questions.
Oh, how she hated this feeling.
Oh, how she could have thrown those shoes away.
But her feet hurt
And they have disgusting blisters now
From wearing shoes that were so tight.
But she was forced to fit into roles
That weren't meant for her
To save those who just couldn't walk in the first place.

She was told to be human quite often
To learn how to empathize with others
And express herself through communication.

They don't know how she became a pro
At being an alien
And leaving this world
And its nuisances behind.

Never apologize
For the way your mind works.

Never apologize
For the way you feel today and every day.

Never apologize
For apologizing too much.

Apologies are for big mistakes
And you, my dear…
You are not a mistake.

She just needs more time
Just five more minutes in the morning
To make up fake scenarios in her head
To feel the tiniest bit alive.

You prefer to walk in aimless circles
With that blank stare in your eyes
Hoping she would understand
What goes on inside your head.

With all this confusion
Life feels like a maze around you
And all she needs is a little exchange.

Without your words
She's just tired of trying to keep you close
And it looks like she's about to give up.

Man, she loves acting oblivious.
It's a performance
Just pretending she doesn't know a thing
So she can clasp your belittling lies
Tangled like insects in a web.

It's a skill.
Watch her uncover the truth
Through your actions.
She spoke very little anyway.
There's no need for words.
She's good at observing
And her remarks tend to be 99% accurate.
Be that 1% and prove her wrong.
I dare you.

Don't count on her
To heal your wounds.

Just count the days
Until she's gone.

She doesn't want to be here
She feels like a burden
(Because she was always reminded that she was.)

Why do people find it okay
To dump their problems on her?

How does she tell them politely
That she doesn't have the energy?

She can listen
But sometimes she can't help.

Take a moment to look at her
She's already a mess.

She likes people who try
Even if things don't work out.
At least she would know you tried.

She's an empath.
Understanding others
Is one step closer
To healing.

"I want you to know that I'm never leaving… I promise."

This is what you said
A few days before you left.
She was so in the moment
Paying attention to each word uttered
Because you conveyed the message
And validated your sentiment with a promise.

Moving forward
Words meant nothing to her.
Neither did promises.

As soon as you cut her off when she talks
That's when she stops talking completely.

Why were we rushing to grow up?
What were we thinking?

Slow down, silly!

You know what the inability to articulate your feelings feels like?

Like being strangled
And thrown into the ocean
To drown in your silence.

Not everyone who claims to have your back actually has your back.
Learn to rely on yourself, not on others.
It took her a while to figure out that there is no one to catch her
When
    she
        falls.

She would have given you the world
In tiny little pieces
Crumpled into the palm of her hand
Because that was all she was able to give.
Other pieces of the puzzle were just lost
And never recovered.

You won't get a gold star
For keeping your mouth shut.

Don't count on people to make you feel good
Because most people have cruel intentions.
That's just her perspective.
It's been a while, and it hasn't changed.

Do you know what makes her feel good?
Some lo-fi music
And writing passages of this book.

Find what makes you feel good
A place
A person
A song
Anything…

She's homesick
But she doesn't know where home is.

Loss of interest
In things she used to enjoy.
Her spark is fading.
Hand her a lighter!

She was told to stop thinking too much about herself
And to start considering others' wants and needs.
Little did they know
Her inward vision is impaired.

You shouldn't fear losing someone
If you're starting to feel
Like you're losing yourself.
She learned this the hard way.

You must let some people go
Even if that means all of them.
Just make sure they close the door
On their way out.

This feeling of dissociation
Makes her feel like she's not living
In the same lifetime as everybody else.

It's the strength of those
Who cry themselves to sleep
While still being hopeful
For a better tomorrow.

She's making progress
And she's the only one who is proud of herself.

Whenever it feels like she's at her lowest
Her feet can't bear the weight of her body.
She can't get out of bed
And she certainly can't run to anyone for help.
Please get her some crutches.

Once assistance is provided
Suddenly, she's mute.

She Got the Memo

She was used to living a lonesome life, without a close circle of friends and with no favorite family member to rely on. She tried to attend events, functions, and stupid weddings to enhance her social skills… to get to know more people… to make friends. With time, she gained not one but two friends who she felt were close to her like the grains of sand. They shared secrets, the deep kind. Dark humor and banter were the foundation of their friendship. With time, she realized that it wasn't all jokes. They were telling the truth, and her stupid mind was slow to comprehend that all those harmful "jokes" hid a little bit of truth. But she tried hard to keep the bond. She did this by giving her friends what they needed: money, car rides, pleasure… you name it. Until she realized that one day, they got what they wanted out of the friendship, got bored, and blocked her. She got the not-so-hidden message.

It's a complete mess.
Her mind.
Her mind's a complete mess.

In the comfort of her home
There's no close unity
And barely any form of communication.
She's just thankful that they're all breathing.
Only their existence matters
And it provides
So much comfort.
More than they know.

Being around others
Is when she wears her most beautiful mask
The one stored in a golden box
Within a secret drawer
Sealed with a key
That only she has.

But she wants to show you
Each side of her
But she certainly doesn't want to show you
The misery that has been accumulated
Over years and years of denial.

After all,
She was raised to fake it 'til she made it.

Identifying the hazardous signs
In people
Places
And memories
Made her confined
To her own space.
Her own bubble.

Life comes in different shades
Pick your favorite colors
And see how vibrant your canvas will look.

Even a disastrous piece of art
Can look like a magnificent masterpiece.

You didn't have to stay
If she wasn't good enough for you.
The door is open.
Get out.

As she brushes every emotion off her shoulders
The dark soot that falls on the ground
Turns her beige marble bedroom floor
Into a dull space that feels ike a psych ward.

Time to do some repainting
Maybe add some decorations
To brighten up the spirits
Of those four walls.

Maybe a picture of her smiling
To act as a goal
But she thinks that's a bit too much.
So she decides to display
A baby picture of her
At her bedside
To remind her every day and night
That she will forever make her proud.

Her soul doesn't feel like
It's in alignment with her body.
She always felt out of touch with reality.

It's funny how people save money
For material things.
New clothes,
New cars,
Or a new house.
While she's been saving
For her next therapy session.

Her soul's a bit too expensive to mend
And parts that need to be replaced
Might not even be available
Or have been discontinued.

They used to joke about her being a Gemini
And how she can go from one mood
To another
In a split second.

I think it's just her hypersensitivity.
Don't blame her mood on a zodiac sign.

A: Hi…

B: Hello! How can I help you?

A: Just taking a number to queue up in line.

B: For which service?

A: To pick up my sanity.

…

A: Looks like it's busy today.

B: Yes, it's been busy for a few months now.

A: It's okay… I got time.

"I can be myself around you."

Those are just some words she says
When she looks at herself
In the mirror
Because she knows for a fact
That she wouldn't feel the same around others.

Guiding others
When she was the one who needed
The most guidance out of everyone.

She cannot predict the future
But she can see the light
At the end of the tunnel.
She prays that she'll make it
And if she doesn't
God knows she tried.

You need to teach yourself
How to love each corner of your mind
Especially the limbic system.
It can act like a troubled child.

We change the frequency
When we don't like what we're listening to.
She feels like she's just another number
On the radio.
Don't like what you're hearing?
Switch the channel.

"Open up,"
They said.
"We hear you,"
They said.

Liars.

Expressing herself
Felt like drunk texting.
It feels good in the moment
But is accompanied by great heights of regret
The morning after.

She recalls meditating for the first time.
She couldn't last two minutes.
It's pretty dark up there in her mind
And considering that she's scared of the dark
The weird part is that it's the only place
That feels like home.

Keeping yourself busy
Instead of getting too into your mind
Is the smoothest way
To avoid disaster.

She won't waste time on people who plan to leave.
Let her know from the start
If she's going to receive a short-term contract
That will only last a few days
So she could terminate it earlier than planned.

It's the people with dark humor
Who amuse her the most.
At least they can get a laugh out of
The misery that is their life.

Don't think about saving the world
Think about saving yourself
From a world that is far from saving.

Carrying these unwanted feelings
Feels like dragging body bags
To graves with unwelcoming arms.

Her old self disappeared
And no one knows when she'll be back.
No one knows that she only got a one-way ticket out.

Resolving her own problems
Through a melody that moves her soul
And a sound of hope playing in the background
Like a classic sonata played by a pianist
Which tends to echo in the back of her mind
In a melancholic tone…

Can you hear it?

She always tried to find ways to soar.
To fly away from all the troublesome moments
The ones that she doesn't want to be present for.
But they always find a way to rip out her wings
And leave her grounded in quicksand
That sucks her into a void
Of eternal agony.

Simply waiting forever
For a high enough level of serotonin
To resurface.

She used to have hopes and dreams
That were decorated in glitter and gold.
She had people who made her feel wanted.
Any knives in her back would be removed.
Heck, she would be shielded.

Nowadays, she just feels like a corpse
Bathing in the pile of dirt she calls her life
And those knives in her back
Are thrown and pushed in deep
By the same people
Who have been closer to her than the ring on her finger.

She's so tired of keeping you close.
Gives her the feeling of asphyxiation.

It's getting pretty cold here.
And I don't mean the weather.

Bittersweet

She loves their presence, but she hates being around them. She loves to hear them laugh, but she longs for silence. She loves the warmth of hugs, but she always tends to question the reasons why she receives them.

Being a people pleaser is the norm for her, because that's when people like her the most. Sometimes she needs to understand that she, too, is part of the "people" equation, who needs to be pleased by the choices she made in her life.

She doesn't want to be the builder
Or the fixer
Or the mediator
She wants to burn it all down
And stand there
Just to watch it fall apart
With a smirk on her face.

But she'll probably regret it later
So I think she'll keep this thought to herself.

She managed to pick herself up
On her own
And with two friends
Who she would burn down the world for.

She finds it hard to express herself
So she'll just tell a white lie
With a bit of truth
Between the lines
And hope people will understand.

Cut the "diamonds are formed under pressure" nonsense.
It's scientifically correct
But don't apply it to real life.

Yours Truly,
Someone Who's Exhausted

You don't get the best of her
She does.

She acts banal around people
Just to get a sense of acceptance.
And then there's you
There's space for her in your heart
Your arms
Your life
And for once
She doesn't feel like a burden.

She's been going around
Treating people like loose change
Making them feel so insignificant.
I can promise you
That what she's doing is unintentional.
Her biggest priority right now
Is herself.

Backstabbers don't faze her anymore.
Y'all are just blocking the rays of light on her back.

What a shame
She's too young for this.

A feeling so visceral
She can't seem to take these irrational thoughts out of her brain.
Her feelings seem to be eating the last pieces
That are the best of her,
And it feels like she's being burned by cigarettes
all over her body.
She knows it burns.
She just finds pleasure in pain.

She always used to say
That she wouldn't apologize
Unless it was for a big mistake.

Look at her now, apologizing to herself
For things she never said
And never did.

That's a pretty big mistake.

She did many stupid things in the past
But giving you the world was the stupidest of all.

People tend to wonder
Why she doesn't seem to quit.
It's because she still has that tiny bit of hope.

Fractures in her skull from overthinking
She's her own worst enemy most times.

I need some room to breathe
Just take anything you want
And go.

The best feeling is when you have someone
Who is "soul-connected" to you.
Without needing anything from you
Without daily conversations
You're still always connected.

Learn to fight your way out of battles
That you no longer want to be a victim in.
Sometimes you need a heart of stone
To go for the exit strategy,
And lose some people in the process.

Some people are only with you
To know your latest news
Your latest gossip
To "spill the tea"
And when you have nothing more to share
You'll be ripped off
Like a band-aid—disposed of
With no plan for reallocation.

Eye on the Target

It's quite hard to live with the truth that not all of us are living a life filled with color. Sometimes you must keep your eye on the target and understand that you need to fight your own battle. No friends. No family. Just you. Because no one could understand you like you do, and that's the harsh truth. People can provide their assistance, but you must do the work by yourself. Not trying to be negative or underestimate the importance of people's presence in life, but do not underestimate your own as well. Over the years, I've come to realize that people's mindsets have shifted inwards, leaving less thought and consideration for others. I'm not sure if this is the outcome of some planetary retrograde, but this is just something I've experienced. Focus on building those leg muscles and stand on your own for a while.

Words in this book
Come directly from the heart
And tonight
Her words and heart
Are not in sync.

Writer's block… She'll be back soon.

These walls feel narrower each day
Closing up on her
Making her chest feel a lot tighter
And she's not the same person she was years ago.

Three sentences I hate:
"I love you."
"How are you?"
"I'm sorry."

Thrown away like rotten candy.

It feels like we've always known each other.
Two damaged souls reconnected.

Patiently waiting for better days…

She can't be there for you all the time.
She doesn't have the mental capacity
And she's not too proud of this.

There's nothing more to say.
Save your words.
She's long gone.

She feels like she's being lined up for war
But with no armor
No weapon
And no army to back her up.

Trying to remain consistent
By keeping herself busy day by day.
When this brain is occupied
There's no time to be thinking of struggles.

Sorry I missed your call
Or am I?

She's been lied to so many times
She can tell when you polish your words with lies.
Oh, so clean…

She settled for second place
She was never good enough to be first place anyway.

And just like that
We're a bunch of strangers.

Confession…
She lost her battle.
And yet
There's still a spark of hope.

Dear Karma,

Do your thing.

Yours Truly,
Someone Who's (Really) Exhausted

Now that she's older
She is comforted by the four walls
Of the humble abode that is her room
And she stopped seeking comfort in others.

Hello Stranger

Thank you for telling me I have a beautiful smile
Took me quite some time to reconstruct it on my face.

Based on a true story.

We're not all meant to be walking the same path
She's taking a different route.
Time to change into her boots.
She's heading for the mountains
And it's going to be a little bit rocky
And she might be experiencing some heavy rain on the way.

She is trying to maintain a solid outlook
And consider the beauty of life's finest qualities.
There's a glimmer in her eyes.
I think she might be able to make it this time
By focusing on herself
Without having to break her back for others.

Some say that challenges make you stronger
But they broke her.
They broke her into a thousand pieces
And she's solely picking them up
With blood on her hands
From the sharp edges of shame and guilt.
But she will keep going
Until the last drop of blood is all that's left of her.

The fallacy of constant positivity isn't ideal.
We're not living in the best world anyway.
Who are we kidding?

Her feelings are on display,
So people can walk by
And comment on how such an ugly artifact
Could still be standing,
Polished at the sides,
With no one having the strong impulse to destroy it.

If you don't like the way she is
Please take the nearest exit
Because she's not planning to turn back.

She's done so much for others.
I think it's time to focus
On protecting herself
And her state of mind
Just to feel a little bit lighter.

Not everyone deserves a seat at the dinner table.
Let them sleep hungry.

Heart-to-heart conversation.
She would die for this.

Your aura used to shine when she was around you
But it seems to be slowly fading
As you distance yourself.
You found someone new
And I hope they get the chance to see you
The same way that she did.

Despite the hardships
She still chose to heal.

Some of us had to gain the strength
To clear our minds
Understand who we are
And our self-worth
Just to simply move on.

You're not the easiest to love
But God knows you're worth it.

People assume that she's weak
For going with the flow all the time
Like a dead fish being washed ashore.
But she's just living life as is
With all its beauties and battles.

Ever seen someone try to swim against the high tide?
Most tend to drown
Until help is on the way.
And she was not one to ask for assistance.

Silence doesn't signify weakness.
She just knows when she needs to speak
And when she doesn't.

She didn't meet you by accident
She just needed another life lesson… again.

She never carried hate towards anyone.
That's not how she was built.

By all means
Protect your own energy.

Trust me
You're going to need it.

Iyashi

Here's a new word for you. Google it.

No matter what the circumstances are
She will always choose you.
Between the edges of this universe
And the one after
She will always look for you.

Clean slate.
Clean heart.

She's only competing with herself in this race.
And it feels like it's taking forever.

Faces have faded
During her healing process.
You all never meant to see the new version of her anyway.

Only you get to hear the full story
Only you…

Regardless of the number of people in your life
You need to learn how to survive, strive and thrive alone.

Mistakes are the greatest lessons
But she barely focused in class
And her report card had
A big fat F in bright red.

If you take a moment to think about it
Those who claim not to care
Are the ones who care the most.
They just have good acting skills.

If she didn't like it
It found its way into the trash.
Simple.

Sometimes people do harmful things
That we anticipated them to do.
Yet it's still so painful
When an unwanted thought
Turns into a reality.

Her heart stopped looking for options.
She's content in solitude.

Waking up from a nightmare
Just to be living one.
I've surrendered all that's left of me.

It is what it is.

This is going to be one hell of a night…

It's 4 A.M. on a Sunday,
With her hair tied up,
The wind on her neck,
And a cup of tea that went cold.
And silence.
Just silence.
She would never wish for anything else
She doesn't want the sun to come up
Because that's when demons
Who are disguised as humans
Are wide awake.

Let time stop right here.

With all those thoughts that seem to be creeping into her mind
She should be placed in a madhouse.

Today's aesthetic is all about acceptance.
Wear whatever you like, beautiful.

She's not here to forgive you.
She's here to forgive the world
For what it has done to you
To make you act the way you did towards her.

Dear World,

She's trying her best.
Don't let her down.
Give her something to hold on to.

Yours Truly,
Someone Who's (Really Really Really) Exhausted

While the allegations about her kept bouncing off walls
She never got a chance to speak.
She was always the one proven guilty
With no solid proof.

In the end
There's still a spark of hope.
A chance for her
To make it.
And some room for her
To breathe.

We hope you enjoyed the read!

Find new such reads and reads
in many other genres in our store:
https://sailpublishing.com/store/

Follow us on our social media
to stay updated with our news:
Instagram: @SailPublishing
Twitter: @SailPublishing
Facebook: facebook.com/SailPublishing

For any queries, email us on:
info@SailPublishing.com

www.ingramcontent.com/pod-product-compliance
Lightning Source LLC
Chambersburg PA
CBHW031321160426
43196CB00007B/612